To

SWEENEY AGONISTES

FRAGMENTS OF AN
ARISTOPHANIC MELODRAMA

SWEENEY AGONISTES

FRAGMENTS OF AN
ARISTOPHANIC MELODRAMA

BY

T. S. ELIOT

LONDON
FABER & FABER LIMITED
24 RUSSELL SQUARE

FIRST PUBLISHED DECEMBER MCMXXXII
BY FABER AND FABER LIMITED
24 RUSSELL SQUARE LONDON W.C. 1
PRINTED IN GREAT BRITAIN BY
R. MACLEHOSE AND COMPANY LIMITED
THE UNIVERSITY PRESS GLASGOW
ALL RIGHTS RESERVED

CONTENTS

O RESTES : You don't see them, you don't—
but *I* see them: they are hunting me down, I
must move on.—*Choephoroi.*

Hence the soul cannot be possessed of the divine
union, until it has divested itself of the love of
created beings.—*St. John of the Cross.*

FRAGMENT
OF A PROLOGUE

B

FRAGMENT
OF A PROLOGUE

DUSTY. DORIS.

DUSTY: How about Pereira?
DORIS: What about Pereira?
       I don't care.
DUSTY: You don't care!
       Who pays the rent?
DORIS: Yes he pays the rent
DUSTY: Well some men don't and some men do
       Some men don't and you know who
DORIS: You can have Pereira
DUSTY: What about Pereira?
DORIS: He's no gentleman, Pereira:
       You can't trust him!
DUSTY: Well that's true.
       He's no gentleman if you can't trust him
       And *if* you can't trust him—
       Then you never know what he's going to do.

11

DORIS: No it wouldn't do to be too nice to Pereira.

DUSTY: Now Sam's a gentleman through and
through.

DORIS: I like Sam

DUSTY: *I* like Sam

Yes and Sam's a nice boy too.

He's a funny fellow

DORIS: He *is* a funny fellow

He's like a fellow once I knew.

He could make you laugh.

DUSTY: Sam can make you laugh:

Sam's all right

DORIS: But Pereira won't do.

We can't have Pereira

DUSTY: Well what you going to do?

TELEPHONE: Ting a ling ling

           Ting a ling ling

DUSTY: That's Pereira

DORIS: Yes that's Pereira

DUSTY: Well what you going to do?

TELEPHONE: Ting a ling ling

           Ting a ling ling

DUSTY: That's Pereira

DORIS: Well can't you stop that horrible noise?

Pick up the receiver

DUSTY: What'll I say!

DORIS: Say what you like: say I'm ill,

Say I broke my leg on the stairs
Say we've had a fire

DUSTY: Hello Hello are you there?
Yes this is Miss Dorrance's *flat*—
Oh Mr. Pereira is that you? how do you do!
Oh I'm *so* sorry. I *am* so sorry
But Doris came home with a terrible chill
No, just a chill
Oh I *think* it's only a chill
Yes indeed I hope so too—
Well I *hope* we shan't have to call a doctor
Doris just hates having a doctor
She says will you ring up on Monday
She hopes to be all right on Monday
I say do you mind if I ring off now
She's got her feet in mustard and water
I said I'm giving her mustard and water
All right, Monday you'll phone through.
Yes I'll tell her. Good bye. Goooood bye.
I'm sure, that's very kind of *you*.

                    Ah-h-h

DORIS: Now I'm going to cut the cards for to-night.
Oh guess what the first is

DUSTY: First is. What is?

DORIS: The King of Clubs

DUSTY: That's Pereira

DORIS: It might be Sweeney

13

DUSTY: It's Pereira

DORIS: It might *just* as well be Sweeney

DUSTY: Well anyway it's very queer.

DORIS: Here's the four of diamonds, what's that
               mean?

DUSTY [*reading*]: 'A small sum of money, or a
               present
                         Of wearing apparel, or a party'.
                         That's queer too.

DORIS: Here's the three. What's that mean?

DUSTY: 'News of an absent friend'.—Pereira!

DORIS: The Queen of Hearts!—Mrs. Porter!

DUSTY: Or it might be you

DORIS: Or it might be you
          We're all hearts. You can't be sure.
          It just depends on what comes next.
          You've got to *think* when you read the cards,
          It's not a thing that anyone can do.

DUSTY: Yes I know you've a touch with the cards
          What comes next?

DORIS: What comes next. It's the
                         six.

DUSTY: 'A quarrel. An estrangement. Separation of
               friends'.

DORIS: Here's the two of spades.

DUSTY: The *two* of *spades!*
          THAT'S THE COFFIN!!

14

DORIS: THAT'S THE COFFIN?

Oh good heavens what'll I do?

Just before a party too!

DUSTY: Well it needn't be yours, it may mean a
friend.

DORIS: No it's mine. I'm sure it's mine.

I dreamt of weddings all last night.

Yes it's mine. I know it's mine.

Oh good heavens what'll I do.

Well I'm not going to draw any more,

You cut for luck. You cut for luck.

It might break the spell. You cut for luck.

DUSTY: The Knave of Spades.

DORIS: That'll be Snow

DUSTY: Or it might be Swarts

DORIS: Or it might be Snow

DUSTY: It's a funny thing how I draw court cards—

DORIS: There's a lot in the way you pick them up

DUSTY: There's an awful lot in the way you feel

DORIS: Sometimes they'll tell you nothing at all

DUSTY: You've got to know what you want to ask
them

DORIS: You've got to know what you want to know

DUSTY: It's no use asking them too much

DORIS: It's no use asking more than once

DUSTY: Sometimes they're no use at all.

DORIS: I'd like to know about that coffin.

DUSTY: Well I never! What did I tell you?

Wasn't I saying I always draw court cards?

The Knave of Hearts!

[*Whistle outside of the window.*]

Well I *never!*

What a coincidence! Cards *are* queer!

[*Whistle again.*]

DORIS: Is that Sam?

DUSTY: Of course it's Sam!

DORIS: Of course, the Knave of Hearts *is* Sam!

DUSTY [*leaning out of the window*]: Hello Sam!

WAUCHOPE: Hello dear!

How many's up there?

DUSTY: Nobody's up here

How many's down there?

WAUCHOPE: Four of us here.

Wait till I put the car round the corner

We'll be right up

DUSTY: All right, come up.

WAUCHOPE: We'll be right up.

DUSTY [*to* DORIS]: Cards are queer.

DORIS: I'd like to know about that coffin.

KNOCK KNOCK KNOCK

KNOCK KNOCK KNOCK

KNOCK

KNOCK

KNOCK

16

DORIS. DUSTY. WAUCHOPE. HORSFALL. KLIPSTEIN. KRUMPACKER.

WAUCHOPE: Hello Doris! Hello Dusty! How do you do!

How come? how come? will you permit me—

I think you girls both know Captain Horsfall—

We want you to meet two friends of ours,

American gentlemen here on business.

Meet Mr. Klipstein. Meet Mr. Krumpacker.

KLIPSTEIN: How do you do

KRUMPACKER: How do you do

KLIPSTEIN: I'm very pleased to make your acquaintance

KRUMPACKER: Extremely pleased to become acquainted

KLIPSTEIN: Sam—I should say Loot Sam Wauchope

KRUMPACKER: Of the Canadian Expeditionary Force—

KLIPSTEIN: The Loot has told us a lot about you.

KRUMPACKER: We were all in the war together

Klip and me and the Cap and Sam.

KLIPSTEIN: Yes we did our bit, as you folks
                say,

                I'll tell the world we got the Hun on
                the run

KRUMPACKER: What about that poker game? eh
                what Sam?

                What about that poker game in
                Bordeaux?

                Yes Miss Dorrance you get Sam

                To tell about that poker game in
                Bordeaux.

DUSTY: Do you know London well, Mr.
                Krumpacker?

KLIPSTEIN: No we never been here before

KRUMPACKER: We hit this town last night for the
                first time

KLIPSTEIN: And I certainly hope it won't be the
                last time.

DORIS: You like London, Mr. Klipstein?

KRUMPACKER: Do we like London? do we like Lon-
                don!

                Do we like London!! Eh what Klip?

KLIPSTEIN: Say, Miss—er—uh London's swell.

                We like London fine.

KRUMPACKER: Perfectly slick.

DUSTY: Why don't you come and live here
                then?

KLIPSTEIN: Well, no, Miss—er—you haven't quite
got it
(I'm afraid I didn't quite catch your
name—
But I'm very pleased to meet you all
the same)—
London's a little too gay for us
Yes I'll say a little too gay.

KRUMPACKER: Yes London's a little too gay for us
Don't think I mean anything *coarse*—
But I'm afraid we couldn't stand the
pace.
What about it Klip?

KLIPSTEIN: You said it, Krum.
London's a slick place, London's a
swell place,
London's a fine place to come on a
visit—

KRUMPACKER: Specially when you got a real live
Britisher
A guy like Sam to show you around.
Sam of course is at *home* in London,
And he's promised to show us around.

FRAGMENT
OF AN AGON

FRAGMENT
OF AN AGON

SWEENEY. WAUCHOPE. HORSFALL. KLIPSTEIN.
KRUMPACKER. SWARTS. SNOW. DORIS. DUSTY.

SWEENEY: I'll carry you off
        To a cannibal isle.
DORIS: You'll be the cannibal!
SWEENEY: You'll be the missionary!
        You'll be my little seven stone mission-
            ary!
        I'll gobble you up. I'll be the cannibal.
DORIS: You'll carry me off? To a cannibal isle?
SWEENEY: I'll be the cannibal.
DORIS: I'll be the missionary.
        I'll convert you!
SWEENEY: I'll convert *you*!
        Into a stew.
        A nice little, white little, missionary stew.
DORIS: You wouldn't eat me!

SWEENEY: Yes I'd eat you!
            In a nice little, white little, soft little, ten-
                der little,
            Juicy little, right little, missionary stew.
            You see this egg
            You see this egg
            Well that's life on a crocodile isle.
            There's no telephones
            There's no gramophones
            There's no motor cars
            No two-seaters, no six-seaters,
            No Citroën, no Rolls-Royce.
            Nothing to eat but the fruit as it grows.
            Nothing to see but the palmtrees one way
            And the sea the other way,
            Nothing to hear but the sound of the surf.
            Nothing at all but three things
DORIS: What things?
SWEENEY: Birth, and copulation, and death.
            That's all, that's all, that's all, that's all,
            Birth, and copulation, and death.
DORIS: I'd be bored.
SWEENEY: You'd be bored.
            Birth, and copulation, and death.
DORIS: I'd be bored.
SWEENEY: You'd be bored.
            Birth, and copulation, and death.

That's all the facts when you come to
    brass tacks:
Birth, and copulation, and death.
I've been born, and once is enough.
You dont remember, but I remember,
Once is enough.

SONG BY WAUCHOPE AND HORSFALL
SWARTS AS TAMBO. SNOW AS BONES

Under the bamboo
Bamboo bamboo
Under the bamboo tree
Two live as one
One live as two
Two live as three
Under the bam
Under the boo
Under the bamboo tree.

Where the breadfruit fall
And the penguin call
And the sound is the sound of the sea
Under the bam
Under the boo
Under the bamboo tree.

Where the Gauguin maids
In the banyan shades

Wear palmleaf drapery
Under the bam
Under the boo
Under the bamboo tree.

Tell me in what part of the wood
Do you want to flirt with me?
Under the breadfruit, banyan, palmleaf
Or under the bamboo tree?
Any old tree will do for me
Any old wood is just as good
Any old isle is just my style
Any fresh egg
Any fresh egg
And the sound of the coral sea.

DORIS: I dont like eggs; I never liked eggs;
And I dont like life on your crocodile isle.

SONG BY KLIPSTEIN AND KRUMPACKER
SNOW AND SWARTS AS BEFORE

My little island girl
My little island girl
I'm going to stay with you
And we wont worry what to do
We wont have to catch any trains
And we wont go home when it rains
We'll gather hibiscus flowers

For it wont be minutes but hours
For it wont be hours but years

diminuendo
> *And the morning*
> *And the evening*
> *And noontime*
> *And night*
> *Morning*
> *Evening*
> *Noontime*
> *Night*

DORIS: That's not life, that's no life
Why I'd just as soon be dead.

SWEENEY: That's what life is. Just is

DORIS: What is?
What's that life is?

SWEENEY: Life is death.
I knew a man once did a girl in—

DORIS: Oh Mr. Sweeney, please dont talk,
I cut the cards before you came
And I drew the coffin

SWARTS: *You* drew the coffin?

DORIS: I drew the COFFIN very last card.
I dont care for such conversation
A woman runs a terrible risk.

SNOW: Let Mr. Sweeney continue his story.
I assure you, Sir, we are very interested.

27

SWEENEY: I knew a man once did a girl in
Any man might do a girl in
Any man has to, needs to, wants to
Once in a lifetime, do a girl in.
Well he kept her there in a bath
With a gallon of lysol in a bath

SWARTS: These fellows always get pinched in the
end.

SNOW: Excuse me, they dont all get pinched in
the end.
What about them bones on Epsom
Heath?
I seen that in the papers
You seen it in the papers
They *dont* all get pinched in the end.

DORIS: A woman runs a terrible risk.

SNOW: Let Mr. Sweeney continue his story.

SWEENEY: This one didn't get pinched in the end
But that's another story too.
This went on for a couple of months
Nobody came
And nobody went
But he took in the milk and he paid the
rent.

SWARTS: What did he do?
All that time, what did he do?

SWEENEY: What did he do? what did he do?

28

That dont apply.
Talk to live men about what they do.
He used to come and see me sometimes
I'd give him a drink and cheer him up.

DORIS: Cheer him up?

DUSTY: Cheer him up?

SWEENEY: Well here again that dont apply
But I've gotta use words when I talk to
     you.
But here's what I was going to say.
He didn't know if he was alive
          and the girl was dead
He didn't know if the girl was alive
          and he was dead
He didn't know if they both were alive
          or both were dead
If he was alive then the milkman wasn't
          and the rent-collector wasn't
And if they were alive then he was dead.
There wasn't any joint
There wasn't any joint
For when you're alone
When you're alone like he was alone
You're either or neither
I tell you again it dont apply
Death or life or life or death
Death is life and life is death

29

I gotta use words when I talk to you
But if you understand or if you dont
That's nothing to me and nothing to you
We all gotta do what we gotta do
We're gona sit here and drink this booze
We're gona sit here and have a tune
We're gona stay and we're gona go
And somebody's gotta pay the rent

DORIS: I know who

SWEENEY: But that's nothing to me and nothing to
                 you.

FULL CHORUS: WAUCHOPE, HORSFALL, KLIPSTEIN,
                        KRUMPACKER

When you're alone in the middle of the night
        and you wake in a sweat and a hell of a
        fright

When you're alone in the middle of the bed
        and you wake like someone hit you on the
        head

You've had a cream of a nightmare dream and
        you've got the hoo-ha's coming to you.

Hoo hoo hoo

You dreamt you waked up at seven o'clock and
        it's foggy and it's damp and it's dawn and
        it's dark

And you wait for a knock and the turning of a

    lock for you know the hangman's waiting
    for you.
And perhaps you're alive
And perhaps you're dead
Hoo ha ha
Hoo ha ha
Hoo
Hoo
Hoo
KNOCK KNOCK KNOCK
KNOCK KNOCK KNOCK
KNOCK
KNOCK
KNOCK

7

18148